PELICANS

PELICANS

by Dorothy Hinshaw Patent

Photographs by William Muñoz

CLARION BOOKS · NEW YORK

PHOTOGRAPHER'S NOTE

In photographing pelican breeding colonies, the photographer minimized disturbing the birds by photographing as quickly as possible. All his work was done with the full cooperation and awareness of the refuge managers.

Clarion Books
a Houghton Mifflin Company imprint
215 Park Avenue South, New York, NY 10003
Text copyright © 1992 by Dorothy Hinshaw Patent
Photographs copyright © 1992 by William Muñoz

Printed in Singapore.
Book design by Carol Goldenberg.

Library of Congress Cataloging-in-Publication Data
Patent, Dorothy Hinshaw.
Pelicans / by Dorothy Hinshaw Patent ; photographs by William Muñoz.
p. cm.
Includes bibliographical references and index.
Summary: Describes the physical characteristics, habits, and natural habitats of the various species of pelicans, as well as the threats to their survival.
ISBN 0-395-57224-X
1. Pelicans—Juvenile literature. [1. Pelicans.] I. Muñoz, William, ill. II. Title.
QL696.P47P38 1992 92-1221
598.4'3—dc20 CIP
AC

TWP 10 9 8 7 6 5 4 3 2 1

FRONTISPIECE: *Young white pelicans and their parents.*
RIGHT: *Many fishing villages have favorite resident brown pelicans.*

ACKNOWLEDGMENTS

The author and photographer wish to thank Yellowstone National Park and Bowdoin, Cape Romain, and Aransas National Wildlife Refuges for their cooperation with this project. Special thanks also go to Bonnie J. Ploger and Roger M. Evans, Ph.D., for reading and commenting on the manuscript.

This book is dedicated to George Garris,
with deep appreciation for his gracious friendship.

Contents

Brown pelican.

CHAPTER ONE

Pelicans Around the World

Everyone is familiar with pelicans. They are used as symbols to advertise everything from motels to automobiles. We think of the pelican as a somewhat humorous-looking bird, waddling slowly along, balancing its huge bill above its long neck. But a pelican in flight is transformed. The awkwardness is replaced by great grace and power as the bird strokes its broad, strong wings against the invisible air, neck pulled gracefully back and bill tucked neatly in.

Pelicans are highly successful birds. They have been around for about forty million years. People and pelicans have shared the shores of the world's waters for so long that no one knows the origin of the word *pelican*. The scientific name is the Latin version of the same word, *Pelecanus*.

An American white pelican in flight.

Cormorants are close relatives of pelicans.

Pelicans are closely related to a variety of other water birds including cormorants, boobies, and frigate birds. All have feet with the four toes united by webbing, which makes them powerful paddles for swimming.

You can see the webbing between the toes of these young brown pelicans.

Today there are seven pelican species. Most inhabit warm inland climates in Africa and western Asia. In Australia, pelicans are found in both the western and eastern coastal areas. But of all seven species, only the brown pelican,

which lives along the coasts of North and South America, depends on the sea for its food. Our other pelican species, the American white, breeds mostly in inland areas of the western states and central Canada, and goes south for the winter.

Being a Pelican

Pelicans can't be mistaken for any other bird. Their impressive size and distinctive pouched bills set them apart. The American white pelican, with a wingspan of about nine feet, is only slightly smaller than our largest bird, the California condor. Its pouch can stretch to hold almost three gallons, about three times what its stomach can carry. All pelican species have colored skin on their faces and pouches that becomes brighter at the beginning of the breeding season.

Pelicans are primarily fish eaters, using their enormous lower bills as dip nets to capture fish. After the fish are caught, water is drained out between the upper and lower halves of the bill. Then the fish are swallowed with a toss of the head. Contrary to popular belief, pelicans do not store food in their pouches. Instead, they carry the fish in their stomachs.

Two brown pelicans.

ABOVE: *Pelicans have generous pouches on the lower halves of their bills.*

RIGHT: *The pink skin typical of courting brown pelicans is fading around the eyes of this brown pelican.*

While some pelican species eat fish that weigh over a pound, others consume tiny fish like anchovies. Strong, broad wings enable pelicans to soar on warm air rising from the land, making it possible to travel long distances without using a lot of energy beating their wings. Pelicans may travel more than a hundred miles a day looking for food.

Pelicans can travel long distances soaring on the breeze.

Two mated brown pelicans expand their pouches as they meet at the nest.

The pelican's pouch has other uses besides capturing fish. When the bird gets too hot, it opens its bill and flutters the sides of its pouch. This fluttering keeps air flowing over the moist surface of the pouch. Water evaporates from the surface, cooling it just the way evaporating sweat cools our skin. The pouch is also used as a signal during the breeding season. When mates meet after an absence, they often distend their pouches while making soft grunting sounds.

A colony of white pelicans.

Pelicans can live for a long time. One zoo pelican lived to be fifty-four years old, and it is thought that wild birds commonly survive for fifteen to twenty-five years.

Pelican Family Life

Tropical species can nest at any time of the year, but only when the food supply is abundant. The two American species usually breed in the late winter or early spring, when the weather warms up.

The male is slightly larger than the female. Each species

has its own courtship behavior that brings the male and female together. Pelicans nest in colonies that often include thousands of nests. Individuals of some species lay two eggs, while others produce three. The eggs are laid over a period of a few days so that one chick hatches two or three days before the next. The eggs need to be kept warm for the chicks to develop. When a parent pelican is incubating the eggs, it places them under its feet. The feet have many blood vessels that carry warm blood, which aids in incubating the eggs.

Pelican chicks are completely featherless when they hatch, so they need to stay in the nest with a parent to keep them warm. The parents take turns brooding the young and fishing. Around the time the chicks begin to fly, the parents stop feeding them and they are on their own. At this time, they sometimes weigh even more than their parents, because of extra fat stored in their bodies. The fat supplies their energy needs while they learn how to fish for themselves.

A newly hatched white pelican chick struggles free of its shell.

CHAPTER TWO

Life of the Brown Pelican

The brown pelican, *Pelecanus occidentalis,* is the smallest member of the family, with a seven-and-a-half-foot wingspan. This species is familiar to many of us, since it lives along both the southeastern and California coasts. In the East, brown pelicans can be found from North Carolina southward through the Caribbean Sea to the coast of Guyana in South America. On the Pacific coast, they live from northern California all the way down the coast of South America through Peru and Chile. They have also populated the Galápagos Islands, which lie along the Equator several hundred miles off the South American coast.

Most birds that migrate travel to warmer climates at the end of the breeding season. However, brown pelicans that

A brown pelican.

breed in Mexico actually travel north to California to spend the winter. Most of the Atlantic birds travel south to over-winter in warmer climates. But some Atlantic birds are year-round residents. While brown pelicans are exclusively coastal, every now and then they are brought inland by a storm. Brown pelicans have been spotted in states as far inland as Oklahoma, Ohio, and Nevada.

Not Just Brown

The brown pelican's color is really as much gray as brown, with dark blackish-brown markings. Just by looking at a brown pelican, you can tell a lot about its stage of life. The feathers and skin on the head and neck have different colors depending on the age of the bird and the time of the year. Young birds have mostly brown heads and necks, while the head and neck feathers of the adults are white during the winter. While the birds are courting, golden feathers top their heads, and they have a golden triangle on their chests. Their eyes are pale blue, with bright pink skin around them. While the birds are incubating eggs, their eyes fade to white, the pink skin becomes a paler shade, and the yellow feathers are lost. After the chicks hatch, the parents' eyes become brown and the skin surrounding them fades to gray. In addition, chestnut-brown feathers grow on the back of the neck during nest-building. By the time the chicks are on their own, their parents' necks are blackish or mottled with gray.

The pelican on the right has the white neck and yellow feathers on top of its head that show it's a bird in the courtship phase. The other pelican has brown head and neck feathers, indicating that it is further along in its breeding cycle. Photo by Dorothy H. Patent.

Throughout all these changes, the feathers on the front of the neck stay white.

Brown Pelican Feeding

Brown pelicans stay close to shore, usually feeding within five miles of land. Occasionally, they may venture as far as forty miles away.

When hunting, the brown pelican flies over the water until it spots a fish. Then it points its beak downward and plunges into the water. It quickly bobs to the surface and drains the excess water out of its beak before swallowing its prey.

The brown pelican is unique in the way it feeds. While all other pelicans scoop fish up while swimming, brown pelicans catch fish by making spectacular dives into the water. A hunting brown pelican flies over the water, usually ten to thirty feet above the surface. When it spots its prey, it tips downward, wings bent into Vs, and dives. As the tip of its bill touches the water, the bird thrusts its legs and wings backward, giving an extra boost to the dive. When the bill enters the water it opens, and the sides of the lower half bow outward. This turns the pouch into a wide, deep basket. The bird hits the water so hard that fish two yards beneath the surface are stunned from the impact, which makes them much easier to trap within the expanded lower bill.

The pelican manages to survive such a dive largely because it has abundant air sacs that branch out under its skin. The air in the sacs helps cushion the impact against the water and also causes the bird to bob right to the surface after capturing its prey.

Diving for fish takes great skill, and pelicans must learn it by trial and error. While adults are successful at catching fish on more than two thirds of their dives, young birds miss much more frequently. Fewer than a third of the young birds learn how to fish well enough to survive their first year of independence.

A brown pelican colony.

Brown Pelican Families

Brown pelicans nest on islands in colonies (sometimes called rookeries). The nests are built either in trees or on the ground and are made of interwoven sticks covered by grass and leaves. Pelicans nest close together, with the nests just beyond the pecking distance of the nearest neighbors. Normally, a brown pelican lays three eggs in late winter or early spring. But in the far South, such as on Pelican Island off the Florida coast, some birds may nest almost any time of the year.

Brown pelicans typically lay three eggs. The first one has begun the hatching process.

The eggs take about thirty days to hatch. The new bird is completely naked and looks more like a dinosaur than a bird. But within a few days, feathers begin to grow.

Both parents take care of the young birds, which hatch two or three days apart. As time goes on, the differences in

Two chicks, before getting their down feathers.

In years of abundant food, three chicks may be raised from one nest. Here, the oldest chick is beginning to get some brown feathers. The middle one is big, but still has just white down feathers. The youngest, in front, is still quite small.

size among chicks in the same nest become greater and greater. If food is scarce, only the first-hatched chick may survive. The younger chicks are not as big and strong as the oldest. An older chick may attack a younger one, preventing it from getting food and sometimes beating it to death. For these reasons, the youngest chick usually dies. But if there is plenty to eat, the second-hatched chick often survives to leave the nest. Even the third chick may be raised successfully in a year of great abundance.

The young chicks are helpless without their parents. The parents cover the vulnerable chicks with their wings and bodies, protecting them from the blazing southern sun by day and the cool ocean breezes at night. The parents also protect them from other birds. Pelican colonies may be plagued by gulls and crows that steal eggs and eat abandoned chicks. Both adult and young pelicans from nearby

Pelicans protect their young from many dangers.

nests may also attack the chicks. If an older chick dies, the younger ones in the nest have a better chance of surviving. By having the extra chicks, a breeding pair of brown pelicans increases its chances of raising at least one young bird.

The chicks are very demanding. When a parent returns from fishing, it regurgitates fish to feed them. When the chicks are small, the parent deposits the partially digested food into the nest where the chicks can pick it up. Later on, a chick feeds directly from the parent's bill, sticking its head and neck into the parent's mouth to gobble down the food.

The chicks are covered with white down feathers by the time they are two to three weeks old. They keep their downy coats until they are quite large, and many people mistakenly identify them as young white pelicans. The feathers help protect the chicks from heat and cold, so their parents don't need to brood them all the time. Gradually, the parents spend less and less time at the nest. By the time the chicks are twenty-five to thirty days old, the parents return only to feed them. The young birds take wing at about ten weeks of age. No one knows for sure whether the parents feed them once they can fly.

Brown Pelicans and People

While many people admire the brown pelican for its graceful flight and breathtaking dives, others view it as a pest. Fishermen sometimes curse pelicans, mistakenly believing that

Gulls like these may nest on the same islands as the pelicans they prey on.

Two pelican chicks at their nest. Note that the older chick has a fish in its mouth.

they compete for fish. The vast majority of fish eaten by pelicans are "rough fish," those that humans discard. Atlantic brown pelicans consume mostly menhaden, a large species of herring. Pacific brown pelicans are fond of the herring that gather in huge numbers to breed in places like San Francisco Bay. They also feed on the northern anchovy, which is gathered by fishermen and used to make fish meal that is fed to chickens and other livestock. While fishermen blame the pelicans when there aren't enough anchovies, overfishing by humans is a more likely cause.

Pelicans can also be loved to death. They need peaceful surroundings at their colonies. If tourists, photographers, and scientists disturb them too often, the chicks can suffer. When people come close, the parent birds leave the nests,

A young chick without feathers, like this one, shouldn't stay unprotected by a parent for long.

Brown pelicans easily become accustomed to living around humans. The bird on the right is a young one, with white breast feathers and white feathers on its wings. The other bird is an adult.

exposing the chicks to predators and to the hot sun. Unguarded chicks may also wander away and become victims of attacks by other pelicans or predators.

Brown pelicans sometimes feed while sitting on the water. Then they are scavengers, eating what they find floating near the surface. They can also be attracted to fish struggling to escape a fisherman's line. For these reasons, they often become entangled in fishing line and fishhooks. Hundreds of birds become entangled each year in Florida alone. Brown pelicans also get into the habit of hanging around boat docks looking for handouts. Many fishing villages have their favorite resident birds who can count on getting plenty to eat without having to dive for meals.

CHAPTER THREE

The American White Pelican

While the brown pelican inhabits the coastline and breeds on offshore islands, the American white pelican, *Pelecanus erythrorhynchos*, breeds on inland lakes in the western United States and Canada. During the rest of the year, most of the birds live along the coast of Mexico and the Gulf states, returning in early March to their northern colonies. However, a few white pelicans spend the winter in surprising places, such as on the shores of San Francisco Bay. Like brown pelicans, American whites may wander where they don't normally live. They have been sighted at one time or another in most of the states.

American white pelicans during the breeding season. They have dark feathers on the backs of their heads.

Many white pelicans overwinter in Texas. Notice that their head feathers are white. Photo by Dorothy H. Patent.

White Pelican Colonies

White pelicans once bred from British Columbia southward to southern California and eastward through the Prairie Provinces of Canada. They also nested through the midwestern states down into Texas, Florida, and Louisiana. The range and populations of white pelicans have been greatly reduced with the draining of wetlands in North America. Now, the main breeding colonies are in the Dakotas, the Prairie Provinces, and on the Great Salt Lake in Utah, with a few scattered colonies elsewhere. Altogether, there are probably about 150,000 white pelicans left.

Early in the breeding season, white pelicans have horns on their beaks. No one is sure just what the horns' function is.

In this breeding colony, you can see some pelicans with horns and others that have lost their horns.

About 5,000 white pelicans nest on islands in the Great Salt Lake. These birds begin to return from winter in Mexico in early March and start laying eggs around the beginning of April. Late arrivals may nest as late as the end of June.

In any one nesting area, there may be separate subcolonies. A subcolony can have from two to more than six hundred nests, each about two to three feet apart from its neighbors. In a subcolony, all the birds breed within five to nine days of one another. The eggs are laid, the chicks hatch, and the young birds begin to fly, all at just about the same time. One subcolony in which the young birds are a month old may be right next to another with eggs that haven't yet hatched.

Within about five days of arriving to breed, all the birds in one subcolony pair up, nest, and lay their eggs. The nest is usually not fancy, just a depression in the ground or a mound of dirt and debris. White pelicans normally lay two eggs. During the incubation period of about thirty days, one parent is always present, either sitting on the eggs or standing over them, providing shade.

Starting a day or two before hatching, the chick begins to make peeping sounds. Within a few hours, it pecks a hole near the large end of the egg. It seems that the peeping of the chick influences the way the parents treat the egg. If the chick is too cold or too warm inside the egg, it calls loudly. The incubating parent bird then moves its body, changing the temperature inside the hatching egg. When the tempera-

A white pelican colony. Notice that all the nests are at the same stage.

In this nest, one egg has hatched, and the other has begun the hatching process.

ture is right, the chick makes few sounds, and the parent stays still. Meanwhile, the chick is active, turning its body and pecking at the shell from the inside. It rests now and then, gathering its strength for the next bout of pecking. Thirty to fifty hours after making its first peeping sounds, the chick has successfully pecked away a circle around the large end of the egg, and it struggles out of the shell.

The chicks grow quickly with both parents feeding them. As they get larger, the young birds become more and more greedy. A chick will shove its head, neck, and upper body down the parent's throat and may stay there for more than two minutes, trying to get the last tiny bit of food. The parent may have to toss its head roughly to shake the chick loose. As with other pelicans, the chicks hatch a few days apart, and the older chick batters its sibling and hogs the food. Only when food is very abundant do both chicks survive.

Scientists have studied chick survival in white pelicans. They found that loss of one chick happens in most of the nests within the first twelve days after the eggs are laid. Eighty percent of the time, the surviving chick was the oldest one. That means that 20 percent of the time, something happened to the older chick. It became ill, got lost, or was eaten by a gull or other predator. When the older chick died, the parents began to take good care of the younger one, and

A young pelican feeding with its head completely stuck inside its parent's throat.

By the time a white pelican chick is two weeks old, it is likely to be alone in the nest.

Gulls are always ready to feed on pelican chicks if they get a chance.

Older white pelican chicks flock together in pods.

it was usually raised successfully. But, at least in central Canada, two chicks rarely if ever survive in one nest. The second white pelican chick appears to be a living insurance policy — there to take over in case something happens to the older one.

When the chicks are three or four weeks old, they leave their nests and gather together in large groups called pods or creches. By then, they have plenty of fluffy feathers to keep them warm. All the chicks look very much alike to our eyes, but parents recognize their own offspring and will feed only their own. At first, the chicks return to their nests to be fed. But as they get older, they remain in or near their pods day and night.

Just two months after hatching, the youngster weighs more than either of its parents. Its body is loaded with extra fat. At that time, the young birds are ready to learn how to fly. Their parents continue to feed them until they leave the colonies. After that, no one is sure whether the parents and adult offspring separate or stay together.

White pelicans fish alone in deep water. In shallow water, the birds band together and form a semicircle to round up fish, then plunge in their beaks

How White Pelicans Feed

Despite its large wingspan and hefty look, the adult white pelican weighs only about 14 pounds. Its strong, broad wings and light weight allow it to travel long distances without using a great deal of energy. White pelicans may fly more than a hundred miles from the nest in search of food for their young. White pelicans feed mainly on rough fish such as suckers, carp, perch, and minnows. They will also eat salamanders and crayfish. Eating is serious business. An adult white pelican needs about 4 pounds of fish a day to nourish itself, and it takes between 125 and 150 pounds of fish to raise a chick from hatching to flying.

to feed. Sometimes the birds make a circle and tighten it instead.

White pelicans fish in two ways. In deep water, each bird may hunt alone, capturing fish close to the surface by thrusting its head and neck underwater. It can reach prey that come within a yard of the surface. In shallower water, a group of birds may cooperate in herding fish toward shore. The birds form a semicircle facing toward the shore, surrounding a school of fish. They then swim forward, driving the fish with thrashing wings and feet. A variation is to form a loose circle and slowly tighten it, forcing the fish into the center of the circle.

CHAPTER FOUR

Endangerment, Past and Present

As birds that feed near the top of the food chain, pelicans are especially vulnerable to mankind's effects on the environment. Poisons in the environment build up in the tissues of organisms at each higher level of the food chain. This accumulation of poisons almost led to the extinction of the brown pelican in California, and it contributes to the endangerment of other pelican species today.

Loss of habitat also affects pelican populations. For breeding, they need isolated islands where most predators can't get to them. As humans drain wetlands and move into formerly wild areas, pelicans suffer along with other wildlife living there.

The islands pelicans use for colonies are often very flat and prone to destruction by natural disasters such as hurricanes.

White pelicans are doing better now than they were twenty years ago.

The combination of habitat loss and poisoning from pesticides led to a dramatic drop in populations of the American white pelican during the 1960s. It became an endangered species. Fortunately, there are more white pelicans today. Some dangerous pesticides have been banned. Waterways in some areas are cleaner, so there are more fish for the birds to eat. In Canada, white pelican colonies have been protected from human disturbance. From the 1960s through the early 1980s, scientists as well as other interested people had to leave the birds alone for fear of interrupting the crucial breeding season. In 1987, the American white pelican was removed from the endangered species list in Canada, and scientists have been carefully studying the birds ever since.

Brown Pelicans in the Gulf

In the 1950s, brown pelican populations in the Gulf of Mexico began to fall. During the 1930s, there were about fifty thousand pelicans nesting in Texas and Louisiana. By the early 1960s, they had all disappeared. No one knew why, and everything from disease to low temperatures was blamed. But when scientists studied massive fish kills that occurred in the Mississippi River Delta during the 1950s and early 1960s, they discovered that the pesticide endrin had poisoned the fish. Endrin had been used in huge quantities to control pests in sugarcane and cotton. The rapid drop in the pelican population was probably caused by poisoning of both the pelicans and the fish they eat. Other pesticides, such as DDT and dieldrin, may also have contributed.

During the 1970s, use of endrin decreased. Since then, young pelicans raised in Florida colonies have been released in Louisiana. They have grown up and produced young of their own. Scientists hope that the birds will be able to reestablish thriving colonies in the Mississippi Delta, but only time will tell. The brown pelican is still listed as endangered in Texas and Louisiana. It is ironic that Louisiana calls itself the Pelican State.

Pelicans in California

Breeding of brown pelicans along the California coast began to fail in the late 1960s. The birds weren't dying, they just weren't producing very many young. For example, on the Channel Islands near Los Angeles, 1,272 breeding attempts by brown pelicans resulted in no more than four chicks successfully raised. In 1970, only one chick was raised by the entire colony!

Beachfront development on offshore islands can destroy pelican habitats.

When scientists studied the problem, they discovered that the birds were laying eggs with very thin shells. The shells were so thin they were crushed by the weight of the parents incubating them, causing the young birds to die before they even hatched. DDE, a chemical produced from DDT in the birds' bodies, was interfering with the females' ability to make eggshells. The scientists found that the more DDE there was in the fatty part of the egg, the thinner the eggshell.

The main culprit in California was a manufacturer of DDT in the Los Angeles area. The company dumped large amounts of DDT wastes right into the Los Angeles sewer system. From there the poison went into the ocean and contaminated the fish the pelicans ate.

In 1970, the company stopped its dumping. By that time, the pelican population had dropped tremendously. But by 1972, the 260 breeding attempts by the birds led to fifty-seven young successfully raised. The brown pelican recovery had begun. The use of DDT was banned throughout the United States in 1972, further aiding the pelican recovery. If pelicans weren't such long-lived birds, they would have disappeared. Fortunately, there were enough older adult birds left to breed. Today, the brown pelican is doing well in California, but it is still considered endangered there.

During this same time period, brown pelicans continued to breed successfully along the Atlantic coast. However, scientists found that even there, where the birds appeared

Gulls like these California gulls are predators of young pelicans and can reduce populations of already endangered birds.

healthy, their eggshells in the late 1960s were from 7 to 18 percent thinner than the shells of eggs collected before 1947. If DDT had not been banned, time might well have taken its toll on Atlantic brown pelican populations as well.

Brown pelican populations along the eastern coast have had better luck than those in California or Louisiana.

Endangerment Around the World

Unfortunately, pelicans in some parts of the world aren't doing as well as pelicans in the United States and Canada. Many countries still use DDT, which may be bought from American companies that still make the chemical for export. For this reason, scientists are concerned about brown pelicans that live in Mexico and farther south along the South American coast.

The now-endangered spot-billed pelican (also called the gray pelican), *Pelecanus philippensis*, once lived across Asia. In some areas, thousands of pairs nested in large colonies. But now, a combination of pesticides, human disturbance, and habitat destruction has reduced this species to twenty-three colonies in Sri Lanka totaling about nine hundred pairs, and only four colonies in India with fewer than four hundred pairs.

The endangered Dalmatian pelican, *Pelecanus crispus*, isn't any better off. This species breeds in nineteen colonies scattered from eastern Europe eastward into China, with fewer than fourteen hundred breeding pairs left. The decline of the Dalmatian pelican has been going on for over a hundred years, and the outlook for its survival is not good.

Like other wildlife, pelicans have suffered because of human activities. With more and more people concerned about conservation, there is hope that pelicans will continue to grace our world with their humorous faces and graceful flight.

Brown pelicans are often seen around boat docks, looking for handouts.

Selected Bibliography

Crivelli, Alain J., and Ralph W. Schreiber. "Status of the Pelecanidae." *Biological Conservation* 30(1984): 147–56.

Evans, Roger M. "Egg Temperatures and Parental Behavior During the Transition from Incubation to Brooding in the American White Pelican." *The Auk* 106(1989): 26–33.

———. "Embryonic Fine Tuning of Pipped Egg Temperature in the American White Pelican." *Animal Behaviour* 40(1990): 963–8.

———. "Embryonic Vocalizations and the Removal of Foot Webs from Pipped Eggs in the American White Pelican." *The Condor* 90(1988): 721–3.

———. "Some Causal and Functional Correlates of Creching in Young White Pelicans." *Canadian Journal of Zoology* 62(1984): 814–19.

———. Telephone conversation with author, November 8, 1991.

———. "Vocal Regulation of Temperature by Avian Embryos: A Laboratory Study with Pipped Eggs of the American White Pelican." *Animal Behaviour* 40(1990): 969–79.

Garris, George. Telephone conversations with author, October 15 and November 12, 1991.

Ploger, Bonnie J. "Proximate and Ultimate Causes of Brood Reduction in Brown Pelicans (*Pelicanus occidentalis*)." Ph.D. diss., University of Florida, 1992.

_____. Telephone conversation with author, November 12, 1991.

Ryser, Fred A., Jr. *Birds of the Great Basin: A Natural History.* Reno, NV: University of Nevada Press, 1985.

Schreiber, Ralph W. "A Brown Study of the Brown Pelican." *Natural History* 91, no. 1(1982): 38–42.

_____. "Maintenance Behavior and Communication in the Brown Pelican." *Ornithological Monographs* 22(1977): 78 pages.

Schreiber, Ralph W.; Woolfenden, Glen E.; and William E. Curtsinger. "Prey Capture by the Brown Pelican." *The Auk* 92(1975): 649–54.

Terres, John K. *The Audubon Society Encyclopedia of North American Birds.* New York: Alfred A. Knopf, 1980.

Turback, Gary. "A Wondrous White Bird Is the Pelican." *International Wildlife* 16, no. 2(1986): 18–23.

The white pelican's powerful wings lift it clear of the water.

Index